WILL WORK FOR GOLD STARS.

YAY
YAY

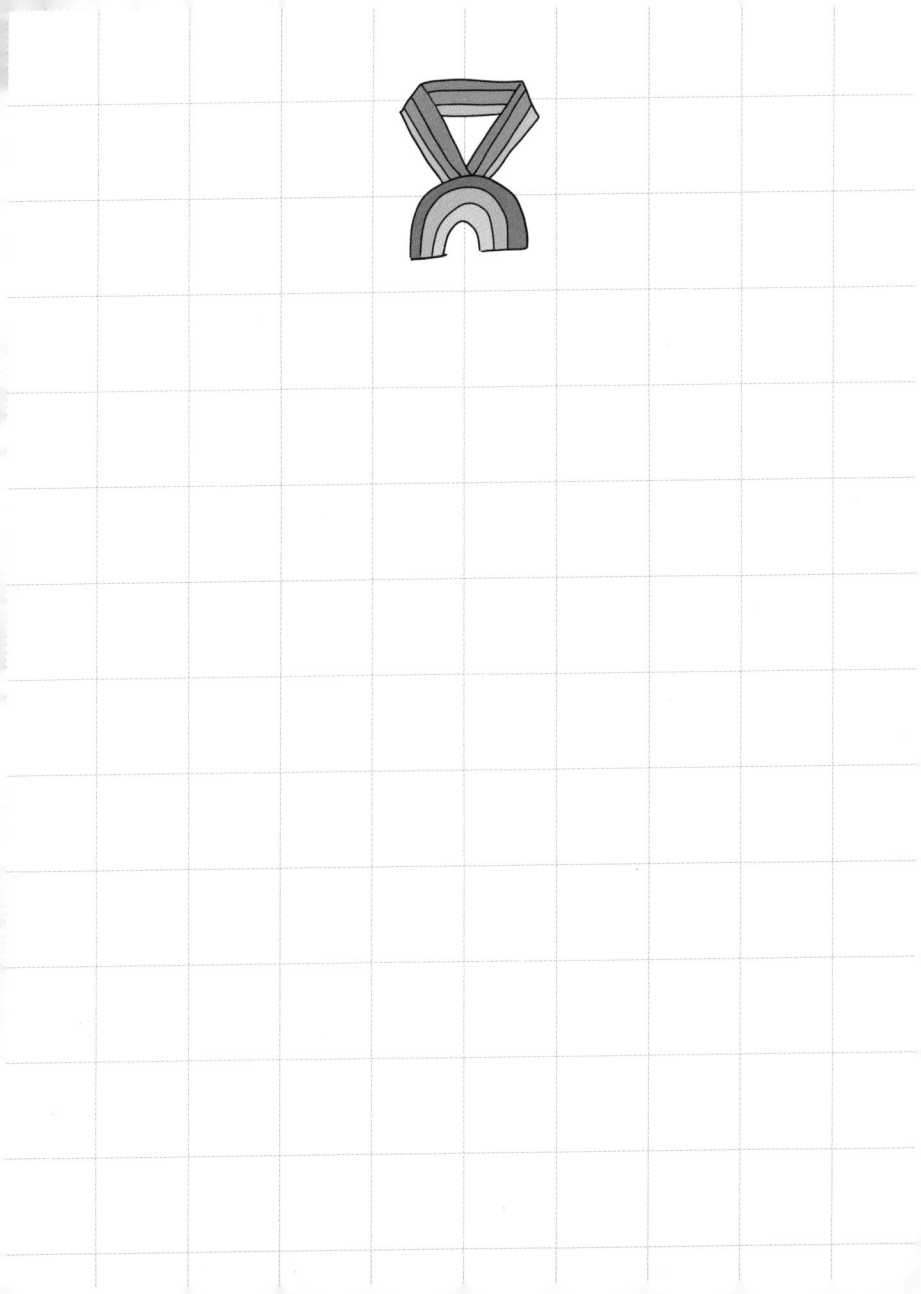

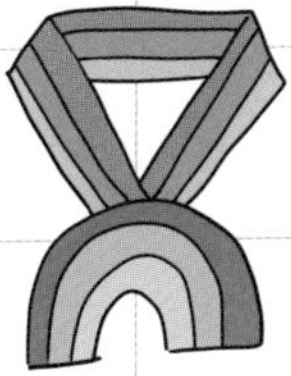

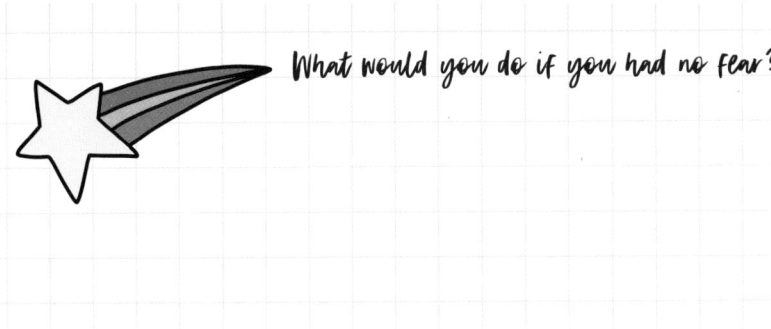

What would you do if you had no Fear?

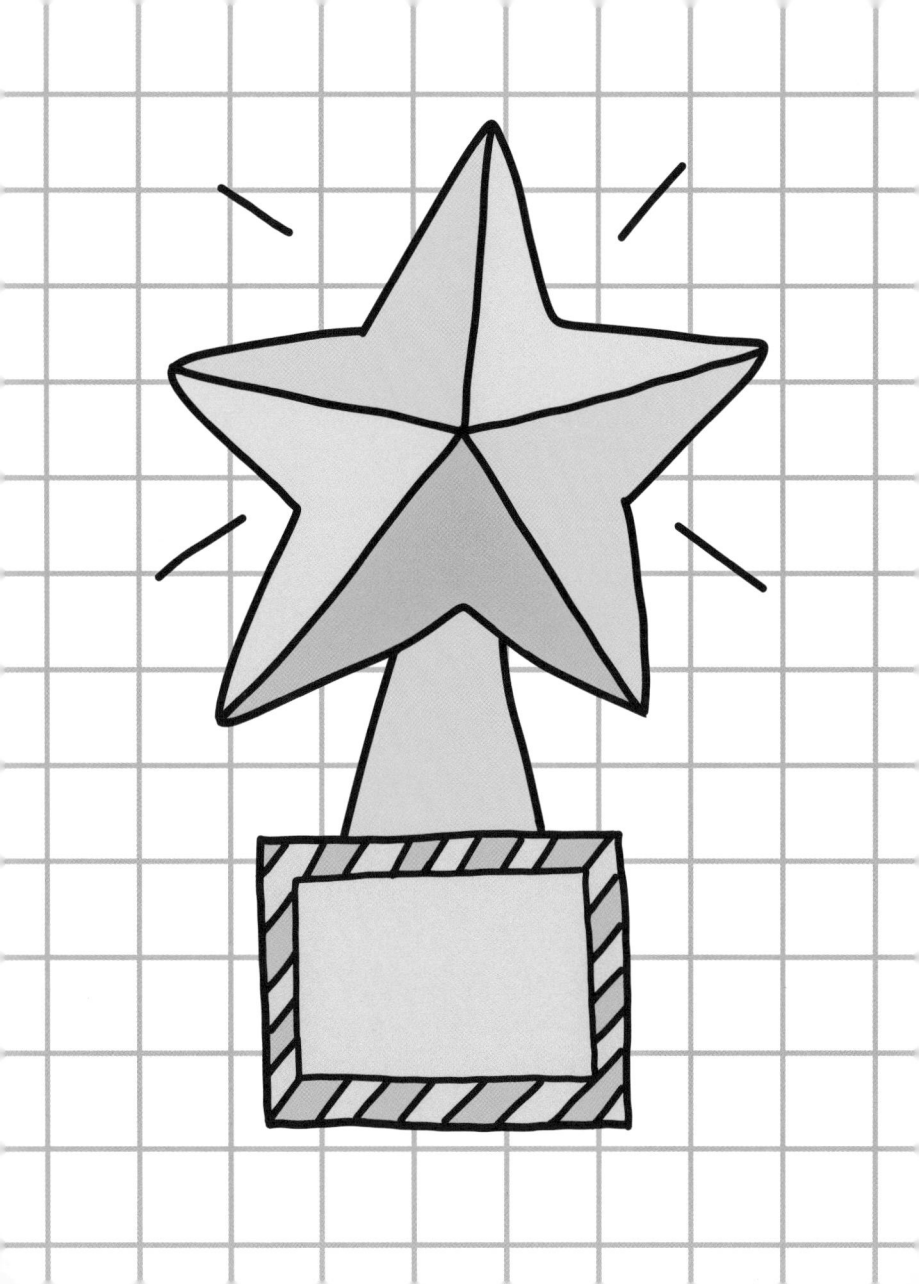

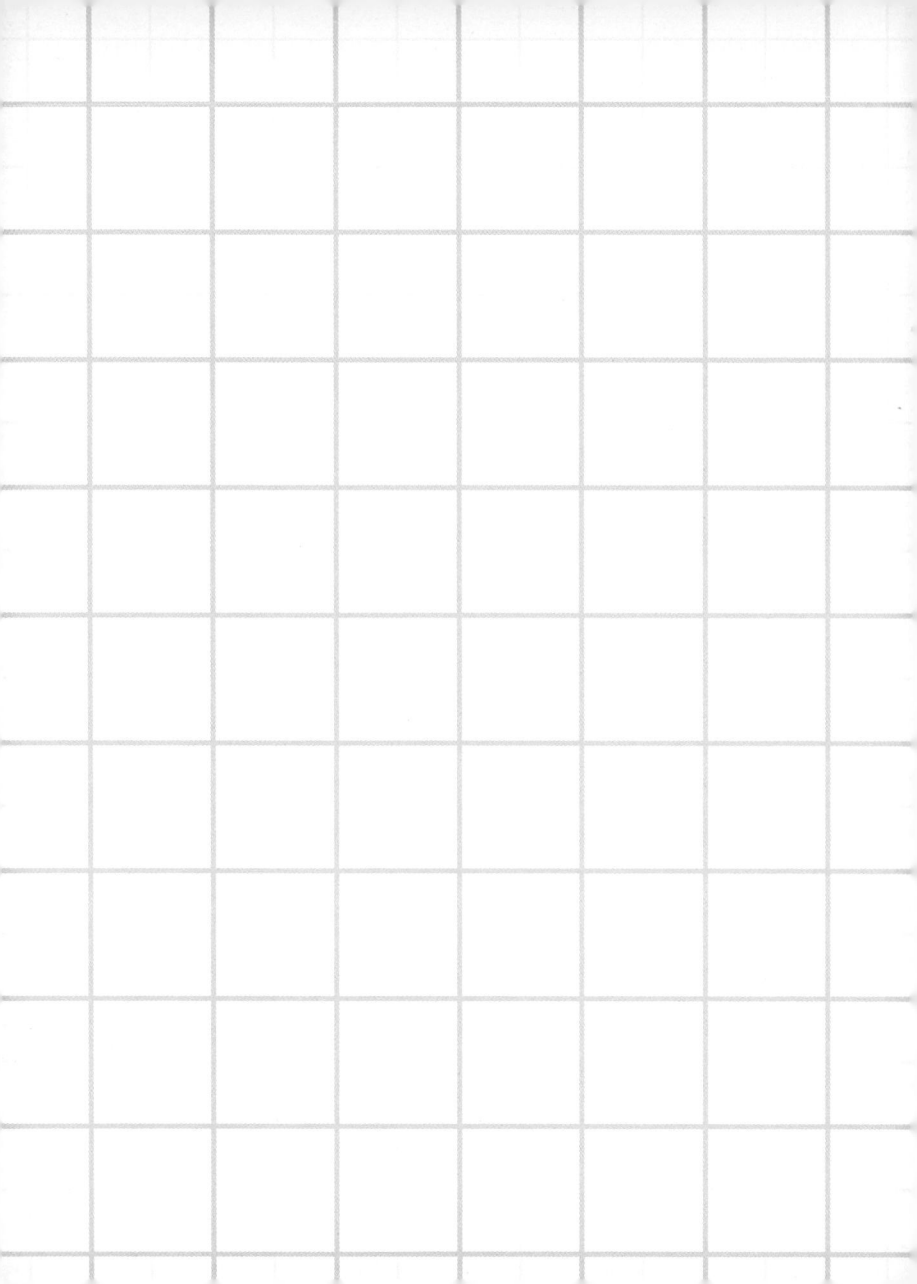

What was your most memorable childhood achievement?

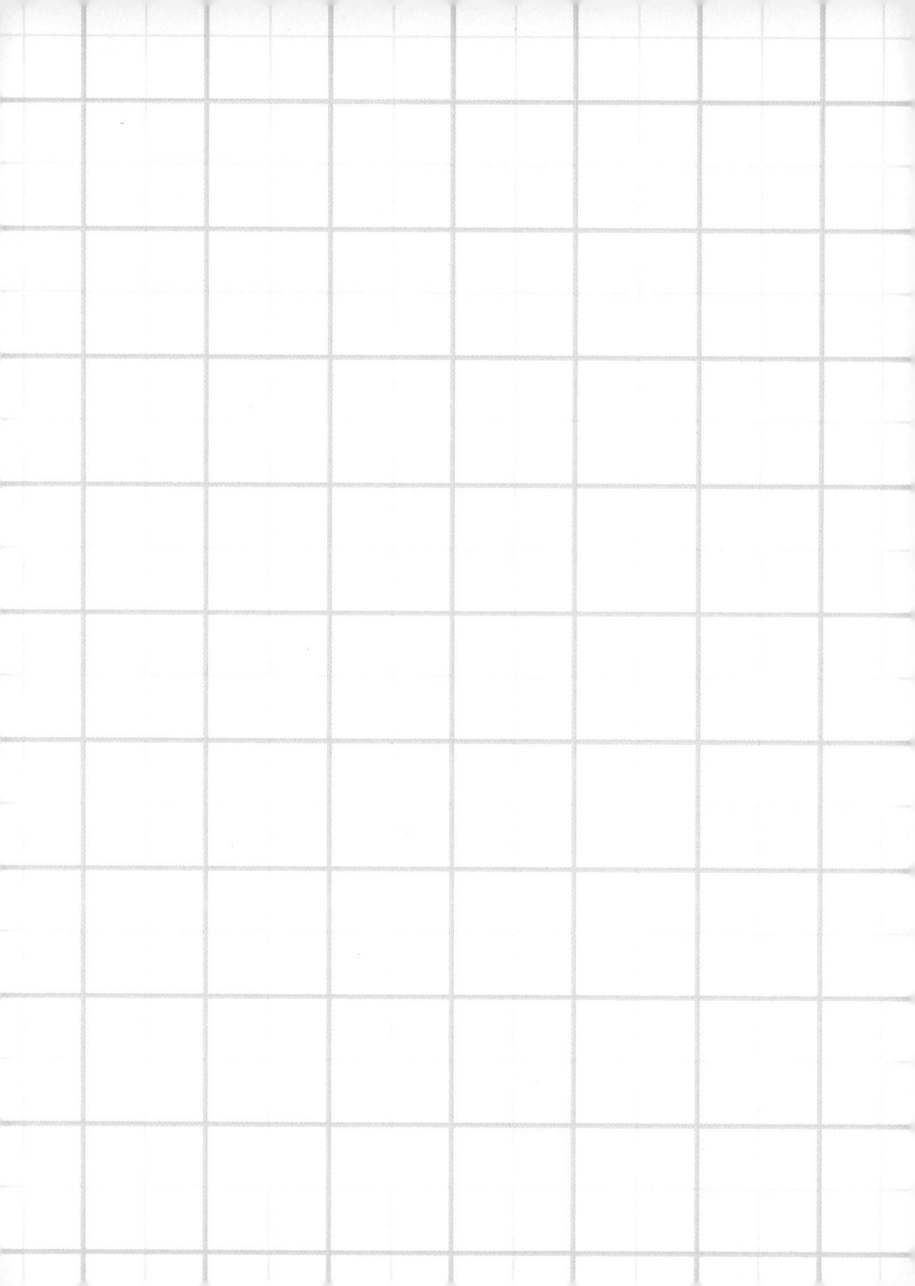

A++

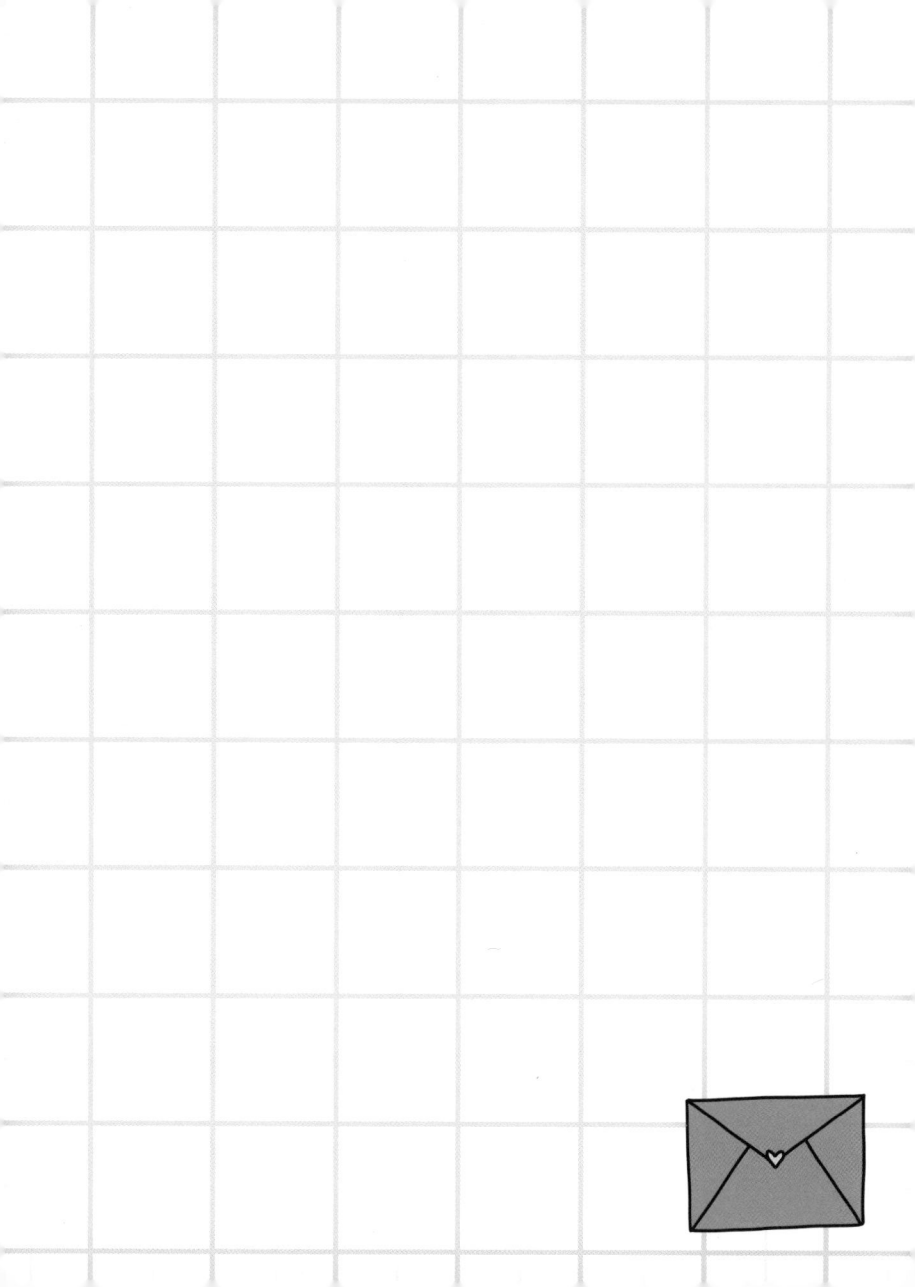

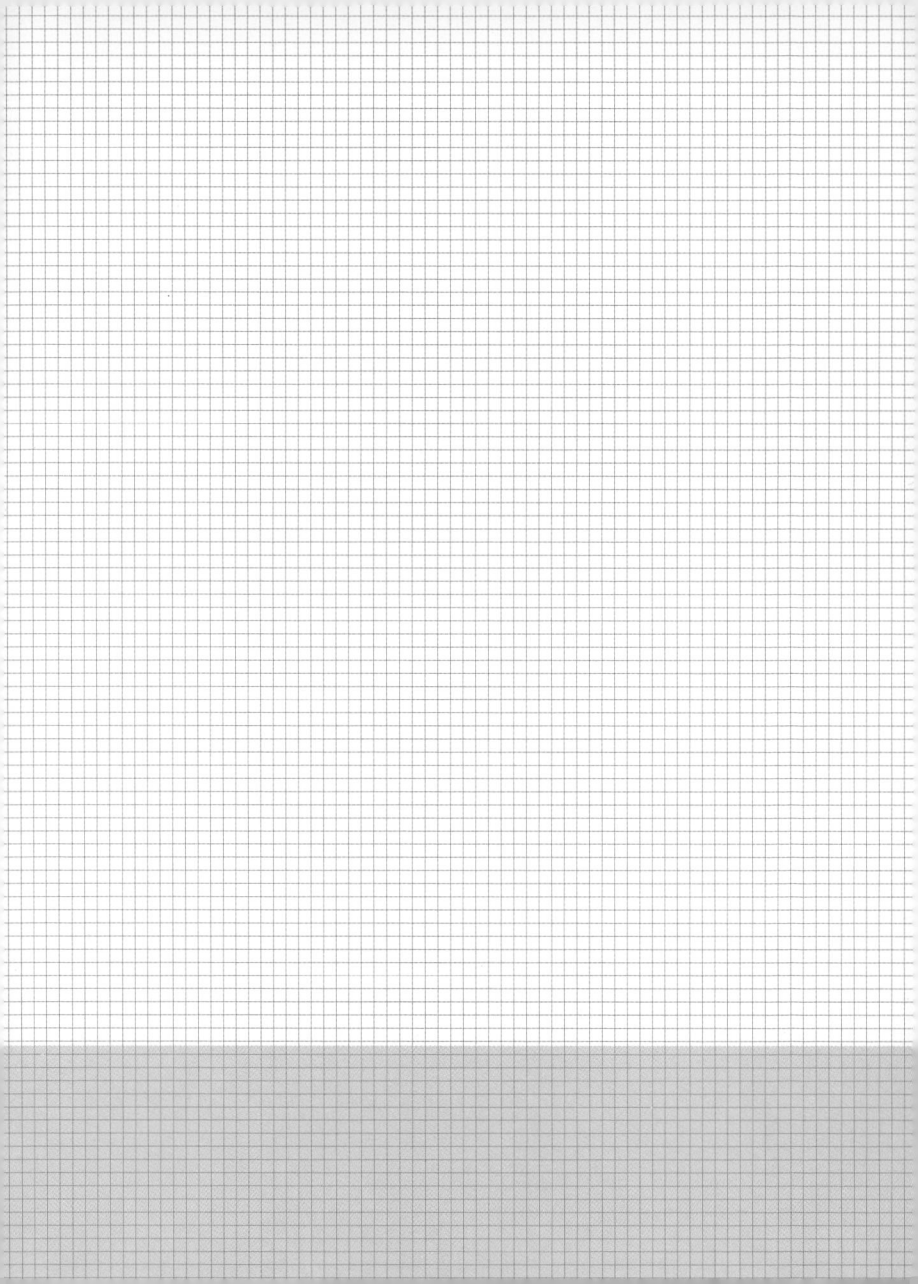

What is your favorite time of day?

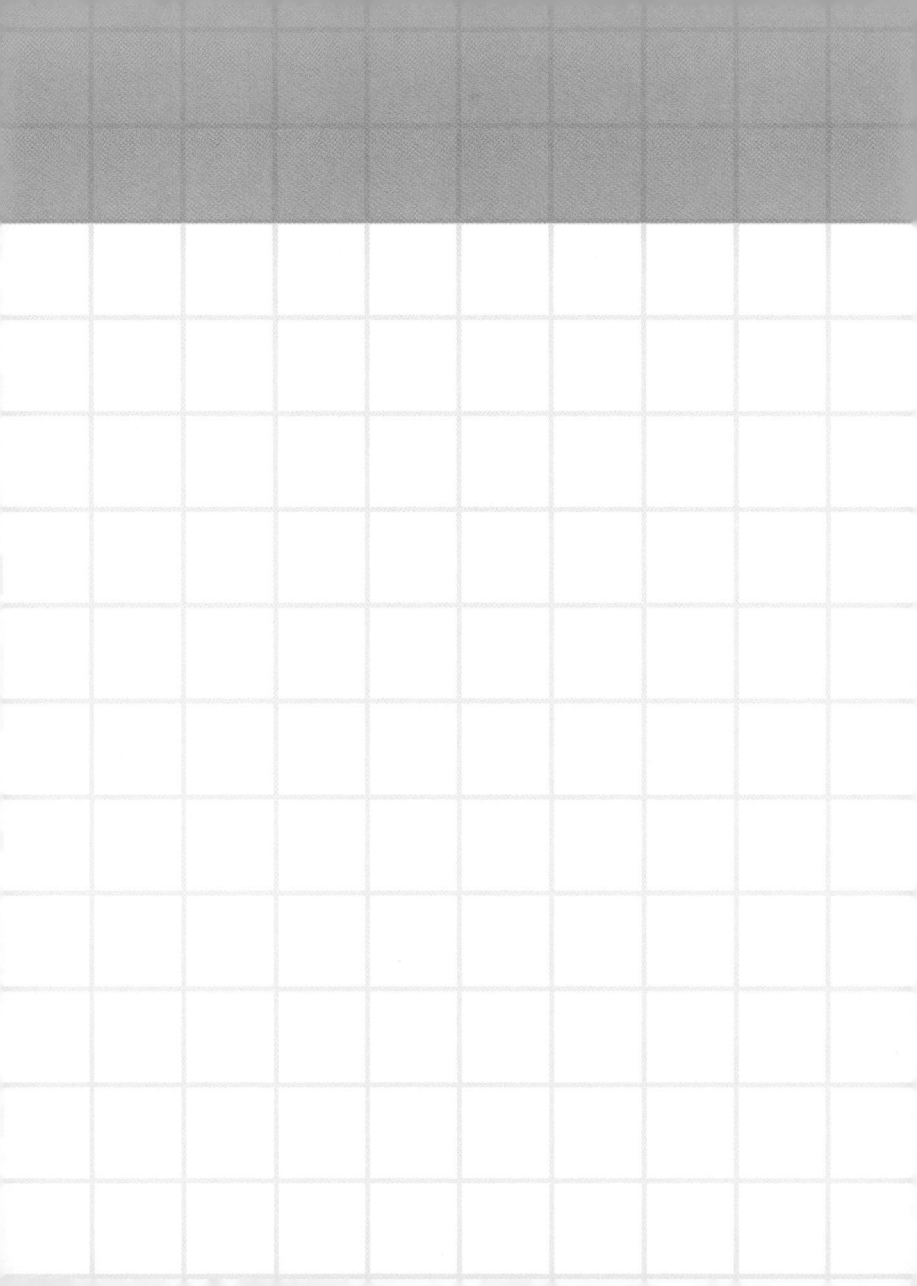

What brings you into focus?

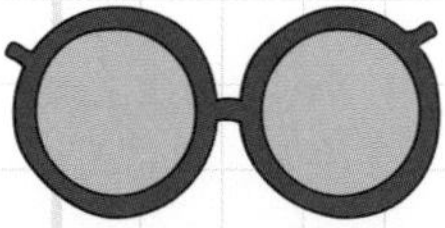

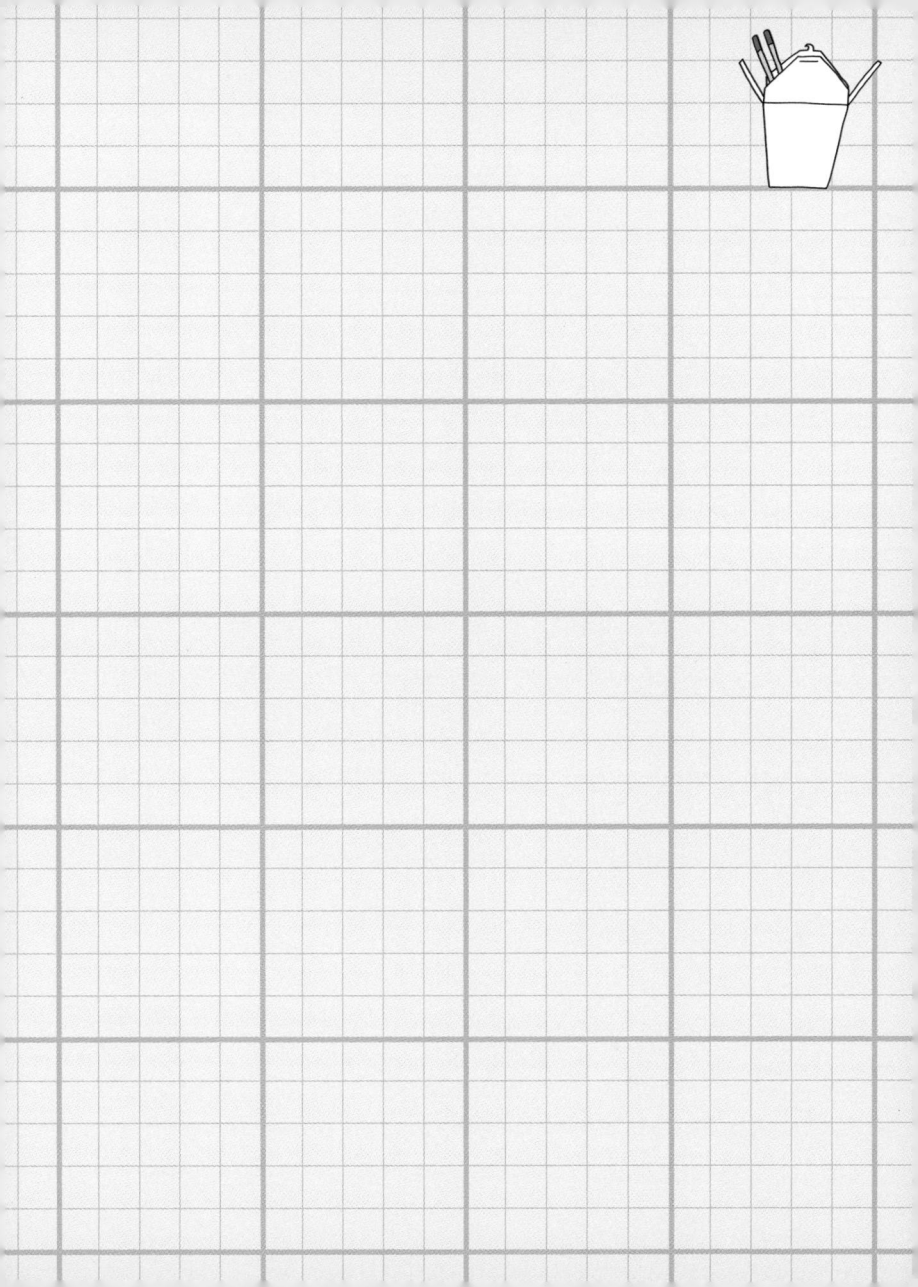

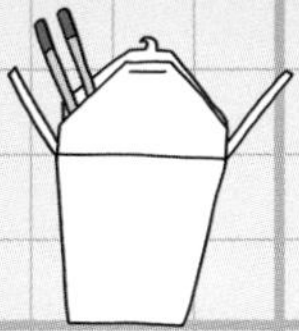

YAY
YAY

What karaoke songs make you feel like a rockstar?

1ST

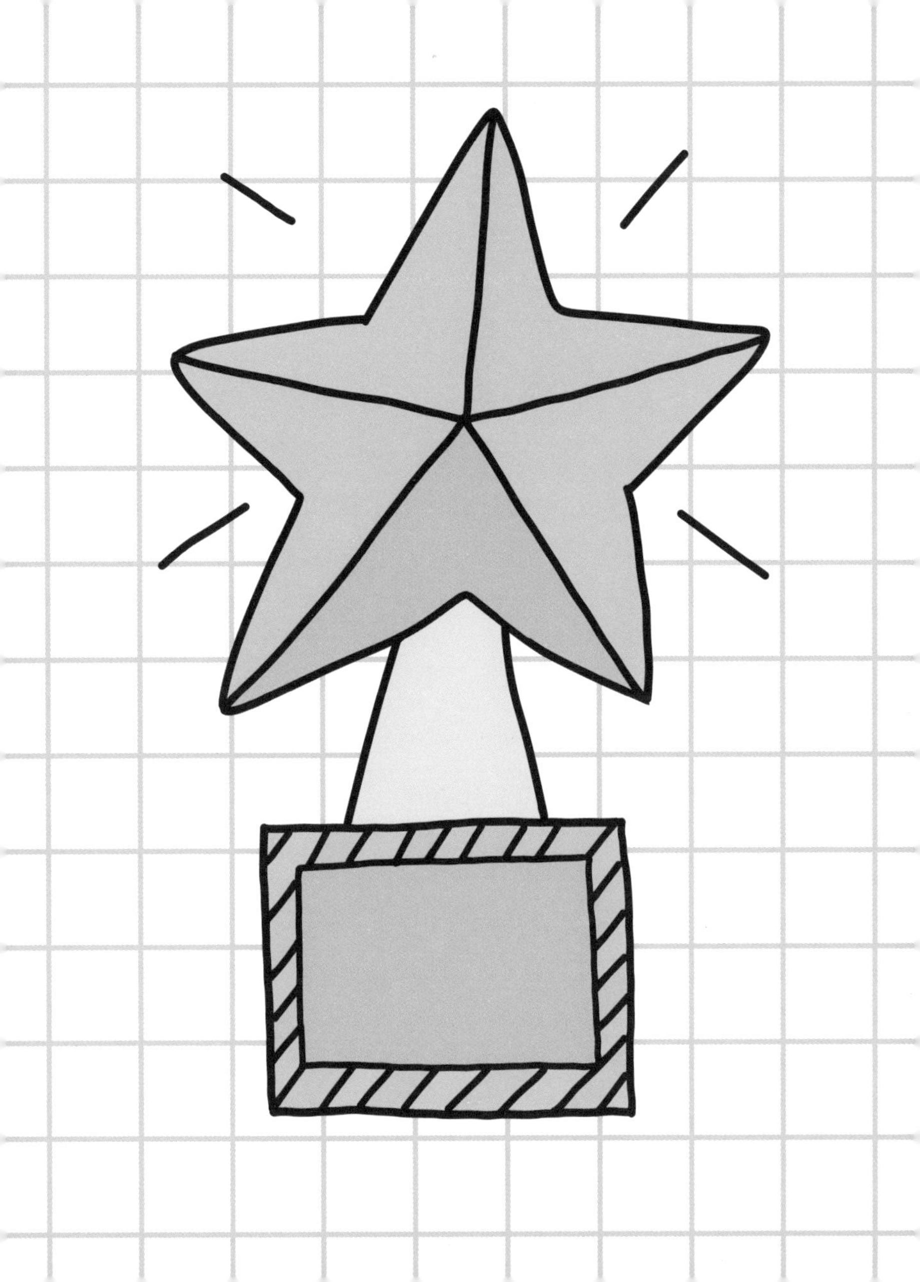

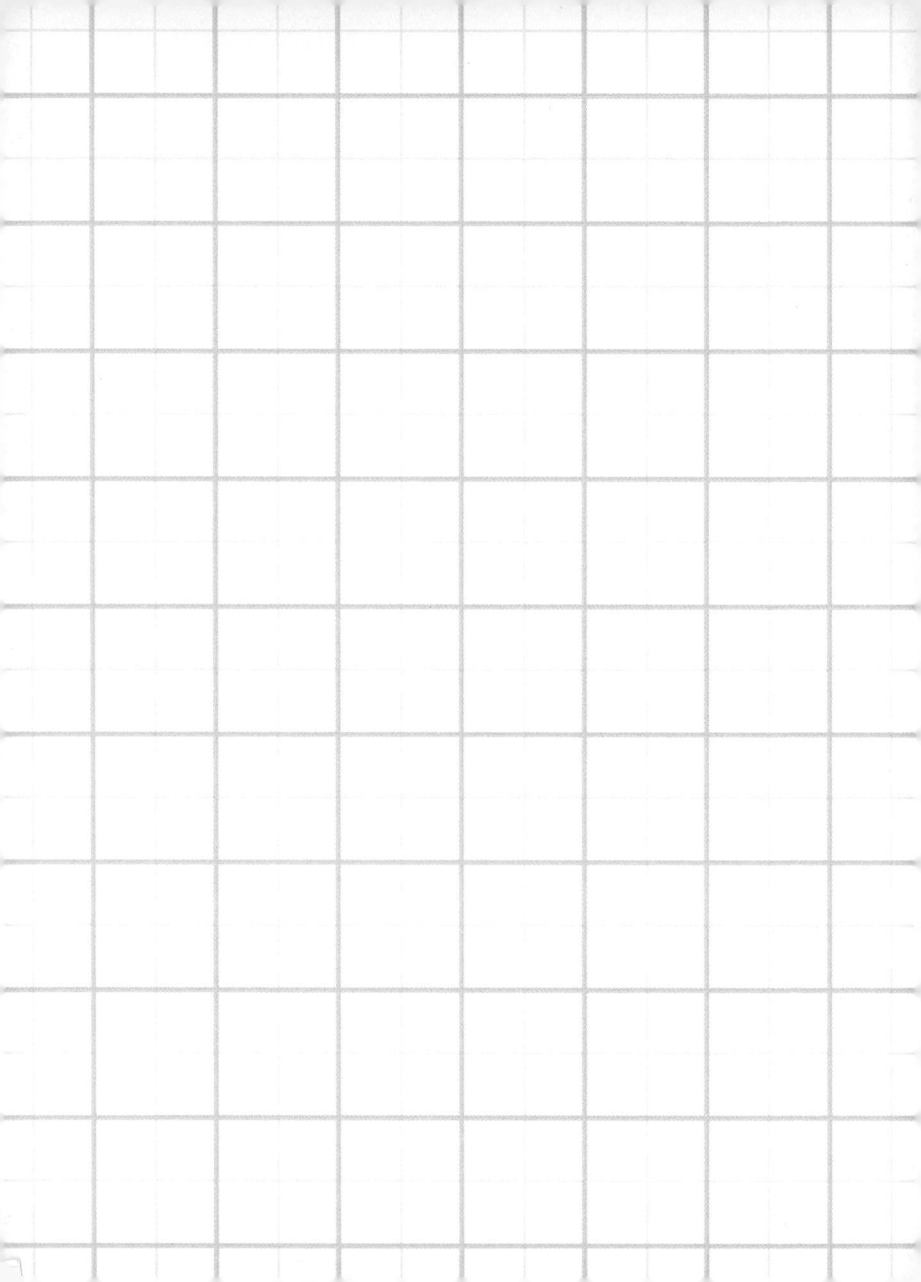

What is your favorite quote?

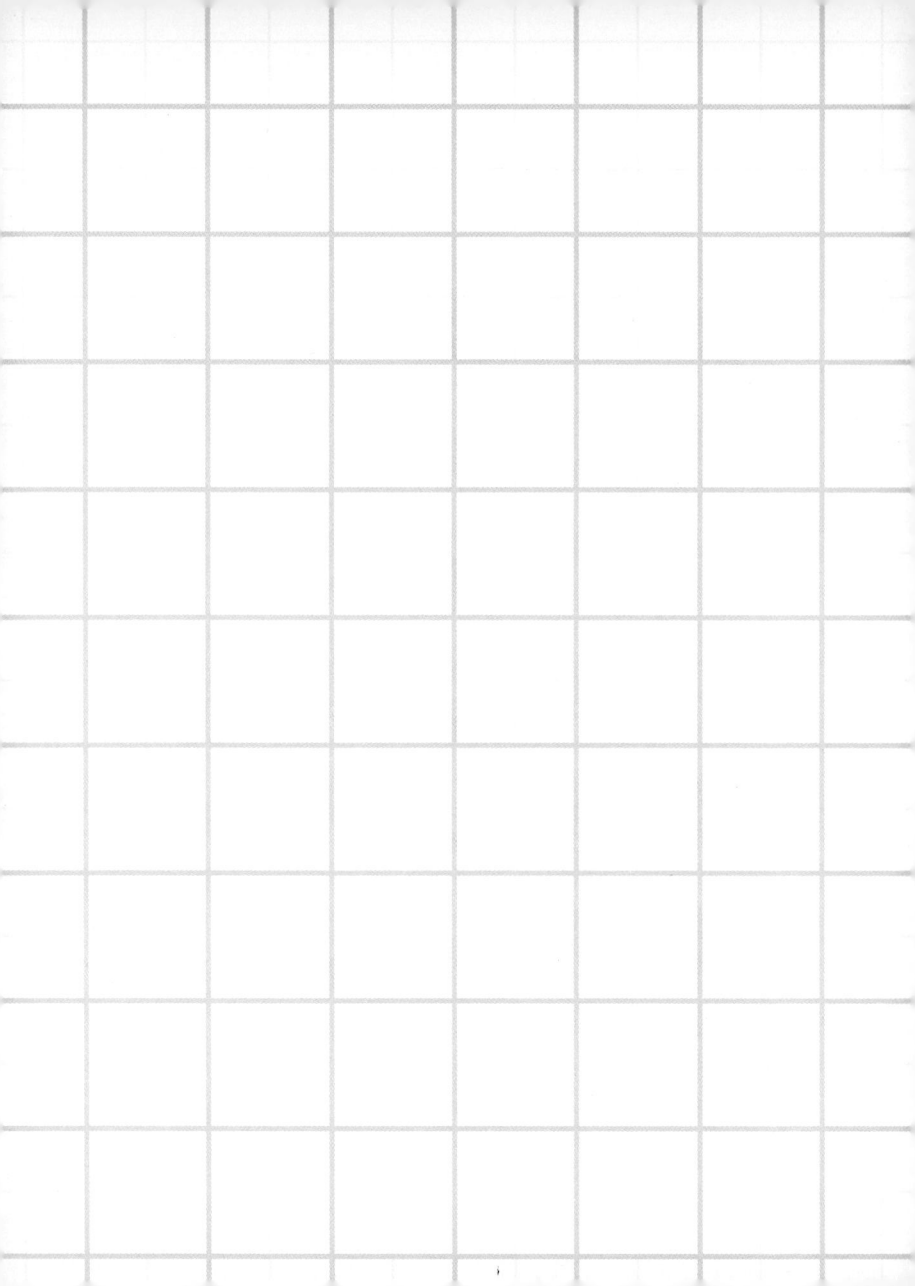

A++

If you had an extra hour in the day, what would you do with it?

Do you believe in karma?

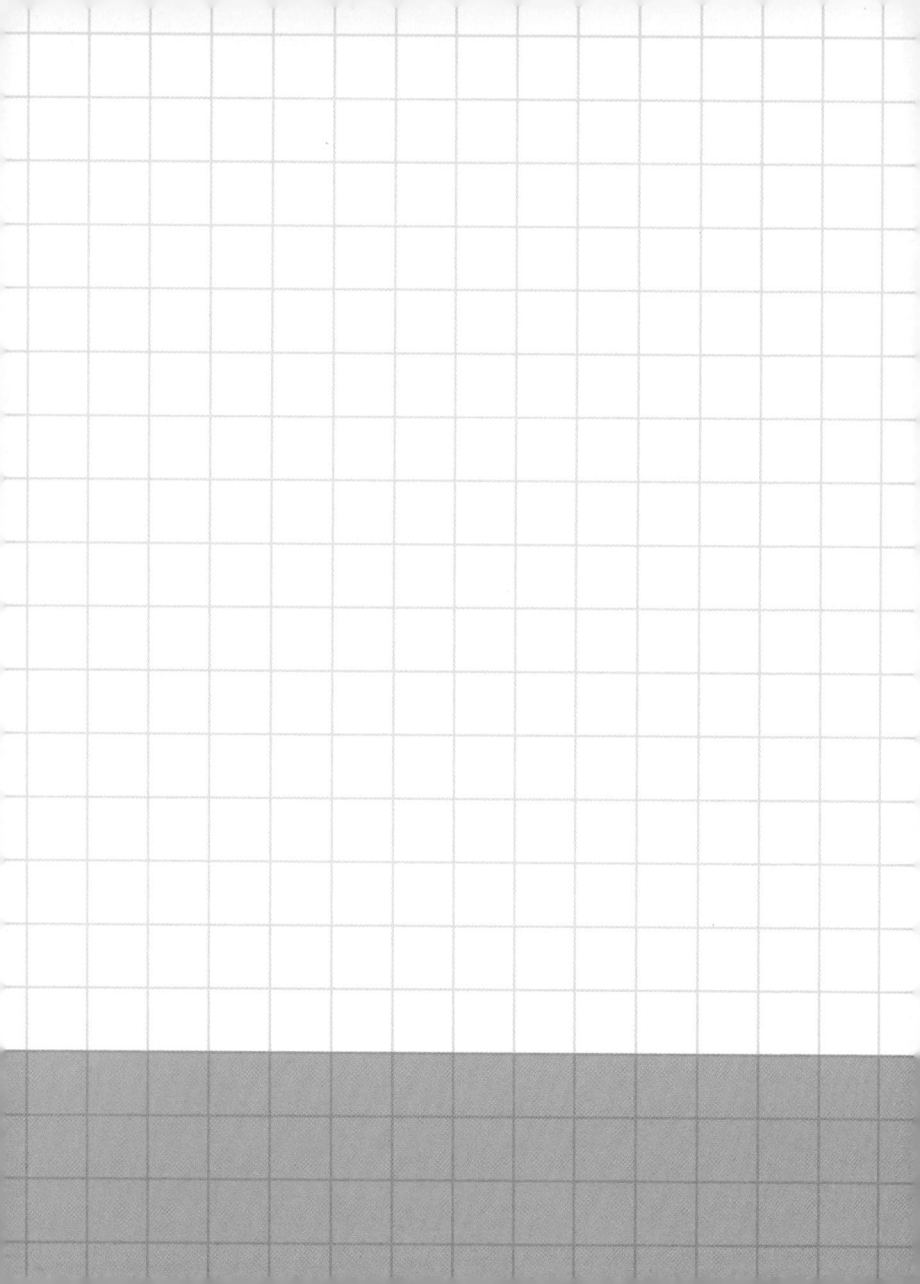

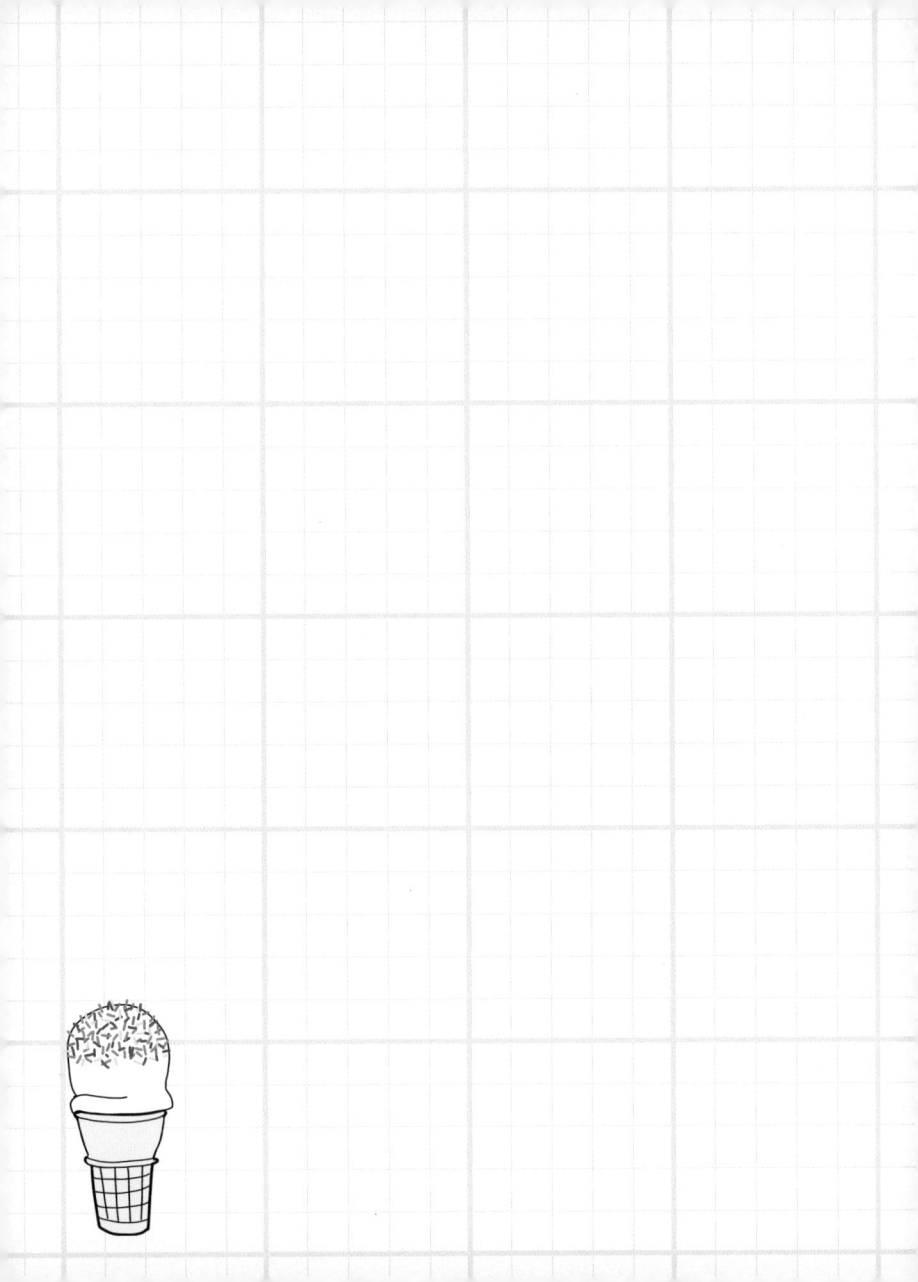

What little things could you celebrate?

Library of Congress Cataloging-in-Publication Data is available.

ISBN: 978-1-5235-0464-0

Design: Maureen Vázquez, Becky Terhune, and Orlando Adiao, with Terri Ruffino
Editors: Rachael Mt. Pleasant and Megan Nicolay
Production Editors: Kate Karol and Jessica Rozler
Production Manager: Doug Wolff
With special thanks to: Susan Bolotin, Janet Harris, and Claire McKean

Send fan mail to:

Workman Publishing Co., Inc.
225 Varick Street
New York, NY 10014-4381
workman.com

Pipsticks, Inc.
1239 Monterey Street
San Luis Obispo, CA 93401-3103
pipsticks.com

Printed in China
First printing May 2018
10 9 8 7 6 5 4 3 2 1

PIPSTICKS®
workman®

Pipsticks+Workman is the collaboration of Pipsticks, a subscription sticker club, and Workman Publishing, an independent book and calendar publisher. Made up of a bicoastal team of innovative creatives, the brand is dedicated to spreading the sticker love through books, planners, stationery, and more!

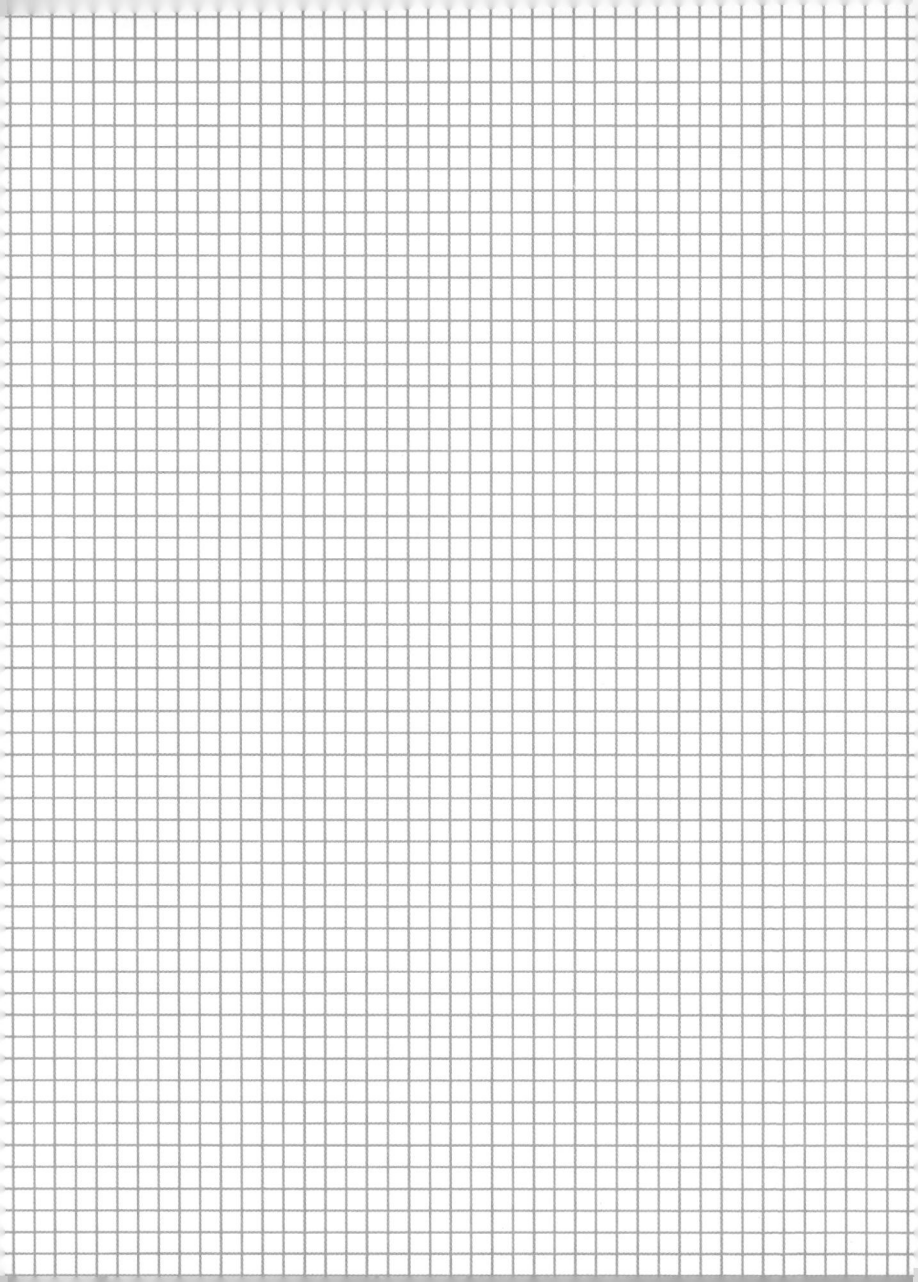